SWEET HERBACEOUS MIRACLE

SWEET HERBACEOUS MIRACLE

Berwyn Moore

Winner of the John Ciardi Prize for Poety
Selected by Enid Shomer

BkMk Press
University of Missouri-Kansas City
www.umkc.edu/bkmk

BkMk Press
University of Missouri-Kansas City
5101 Rockhill Road
Kansas City, MO 64110

Executive Editor: Robert Stewart
Managing Editor: Ben Furnish
Assistant Managing Editor: Cynthia Beard

BkMk Press wishes to thank Marie Mayhugh, Marissa Redick, and Max McBride.

The John Ciardi Prize for Poetry wishes to thank Susan Cobin, Greg Field, Lindsey Martin-Bowen, Michael Nelson, Linda Rodriguez, and Maryfrances Wagner.

Library of Congress Cataloging-in-Publication Data

Names: Moore, Berwyn, author.
Title: Sweet herbaceous miracle / Berwyn Moore.
Description: Kansas City, MO : BkMk Press, University of Missouri-Kansas
    City, [2018]
Identifiers: LCCN 2018036383 | ISBN 9781943491162 (alk. paper)
Classification: LCC PS3613.O554 A6 2018 | DDC 811/.6--dc23
LC record available at https://lccn.loc.gov/2018036383

ISBN: 9781943491162

This book is set in Charlemagne and Cantoria.

Contents

INTRODUCTION

"Spring / is a script you don't want // to read," Berwyn Moore cautions us, but read it we do, along with the other seasonal profundities offered up in her engaging third book of poetry *Sweet Herbaceous Miracle*.

Moore is an accomplished poet with striking verbal facility whose poems offer the usual pleasures of language that poetry provides. But how she perceives the world, her *sensibility*, is another attraction for her readers. For hers is a mind attentive to the small and large detail, to the observation that resonates far beyond the boundaries of the poem. On a basic level, she demonstrates a way to be in the world. One could even say her outlook is admirable.

Moore's poems occur in a natural world that is exactingly and lushly observed and where no human gesture is without significance. The poems are formal, written either in received forms—most often sonnets—or in graceful and effective nonce forms. She is especially fond of unrhymed couplets, the default form in the book. Moore's music is compelling, the phrasing precise and economic, as in these lines from "A Reprimand of Crows": "You wake to new snow / branches bowing // under the weight, yard / and cobbled street quiet // under a creamy skin, / not yet ravaged by track // or tire."

Her focus is divided between the plant world and the human one. She explores both in all their promise, ripeness and rot. Frequently, the herbaceous poems are inspired by a seventeenth-century manual, *Gerard's Herbal*. Recounting the folkloric wisdom surrounding borage, angelica, motherwort, artichokes, and plantains, these charming found poems display a keen sense of humor, as in these lines about the artichoke: "Moreover, the root, if boiled in wine / and drunk, is good against the rank // smell of the arm-holes, for it sends / forth plenty of stinking urine, whereby // the rank and rammish savour of the whole / body is much amended."

At the intersection of the plant and the human lies gardening, a frequent subject and the overriding conceit of this book filled with hyssop, lilac, mulberry, fennel, hyacinths, figs, and gardenias. In "Planting," Moore declares that the act of gardening, of watching things grow from seed "is your miracle / of sod and bloom: the sage and coriander // sprouting, the fluted angelica rising / above your head, its umbrels like wings // awash in wonder." These are by and large poems of praise, even on the occasions when "you planted asters and forget-me-nots" and "onion grass and cockleburs overran / the garden."

In the human arena, Moore tackles illness and aging with empathy and courage, bearing bold witness to the terrible afflictions we suffer, either directly or indirectly through those we love. Among the ailments Moore addresses are dementia, senility, breast cancer, cystic fibrosis, tinnitus, and sclerosis. But despite this catalogue of grievances, she remains life-affirming, even optimistic. At the end of "Breath Sounds," a longish narrative poem set in a children's hospital, a little girl succumbs to cystic fibrosis. Ever defiant in the face of death, Moore writes: "I return to the ward // where I listen to every sigh, pant, gasp, / and wheeze, every cough sputtering with life." No matter how grim the scene, it seems Moore can still summon reason for hope. In "Do You Hear What I hear?" she conjures a beautiful silence to counteract tinnitus in "the violet / unfurling its petals . . . stars // pulsing, dew lifting from the grass."

"Tissue," dedicated to the poet's mother, provides a loving, sometimes quirky portrait of dementia. Here is her mother coming to the table for dinner: "She arrives . . . lavished with every necklace / and bracelet she owns—pearls, garnets, / silver charms twinkling on her chest / and arms—but no skirt over her worn slip." Despite this clownish behavior, her mother's dignity is preserved through her "need for order, / the folding of grace in her lap, the gifts / her hands still know how to make by heart."

Some of Moore's poems are delightfully eccentric and boast a tasty, playful verbal texture. "The Banker's Wife Croons Fear" details a trio of weird phobias—of the color yellow, of cockroaches, and of fear itself—while the almost-language poem "Surprised by Joy" confirms that Moore is a poet deeply in love with words. It starts:

> Surprised by chitlins in the salsa,
> Underwhelmed by evening's empty udder,

and ends with the ecstatic "Surprised by / oceanic hum and warble, by grief's clutch and / years sloughing to now. Surprised by joy."

Moore's lyrical gifts are everywhere on display, as in the poem "Exaltation" that proceeds in a stately parade of rhymed couplets perfectly matching the pair of swans —and the deceased parents— that are her subject. The poem begins:

> When the two swans return, male and female,
> Unfolding and flapping in the cool swale,
>
> four years after our mother's noisy last breath
> and two years after our father's quiet death,
>
> we know at last they are together once more.

Lest you think Moore's book lacks teeth and variety, I refer you to the poem "Dirty Talk," in which Moore lists less-than-romantic aspects of coupledom—the "rumbling in your gut…the tympanic swoosh of too much fruity ale. The sigh. / The snore. The cricket in your nose. A fluky / symphony of body talk." Full of embarrassing bodily sounds as well as grubs, bristled worms, sow bugs, rusty spoons, and backyard dirt wedged under the nails and clumped in the hair, this is as uncompromising a love poem as you will encounter anywhere.

Moore does not shy away from identifying and illuminating the brink of change—of disaster—those evanescent moments when we are "blind and blissful in not knowing," but we detect "the smell of anger and overripe fruit fermenting." She is likewise alert to the instant that "the moment relinquishes its grief." The last poem, a sonnet and a cento, ends with a couplet that proves an apt summary for the collection: "Not everyone knows what she shall sing at the end. / Let what rises live with what descends."

Because Moore's voice accommodates terror and horror as well as beauty it is, above all, a trustworthy voice, one from which readers can derive comfort and sustenance.

Enid Shomer
Tampa, Florida

In memory of my parents,
Constance Doris Roberts Moore
and George Moore, M.D.

Poem as a Field of Action

The weight of love
Has buoyed me up
Till my head
Knocks against the sky.

—William Carlos Williams

POEM AS A FIELD OF ACTION

We seek profusion, the Mass—heterogeneous—ill-assorted—quiet breathless—grasping at all kinds of things—as if—like Audubon shooting some little bird, really only to look at it the better.
　　　—William Carlos Williams, "The Poem as a Field of Action"

I had not been thinking of death
　　　when they stung—three wasps hiding
　　　　　　in the folds of my shirt, quiet as plaid

until the last button, buttoned. Who's
　　　to say this isn't true? What's missing
　　　　　　is the witness, the photo flash,

the fragments of wing and stinger settling
　　　on the indifferent oak grain. I had been
　　　　　　thinking of Voltaire, how he fainted

at the first sniff of a rose, of tongue prints,
　　　how each is unique, yet there I sat, stunned,
　　　　　　uncertain of anything except twelve

rising welts, twelve—the number of stings
　　　it took to unbutton one noisy shirt, fling
　　　　　　it off. And then I thought of Saint Agnes,

muzzled and dragged to the fire at twelve,
　　　her accusers stymied by the hair growing
　　　　　　to shroud her nakedness as she gave

her body up, smiling, to her Lord. And who's
　　　to say this isn't true? Here's how we
　　　　　　corroborate: we all muddle tales, hobble

rickety bridges of time and space, grasp and tear
　　　the scrim of doubt. We seek profusion, little birds,
　　　　　　impertinent facts, safe shirts, hands busy

with clay or bread, and we blunder upon
  miracles of hair and love, honeysuckle,
    a flutter of eyelashes on a wrist—

and we sing—all of us saints, our abundant arms
  reaching toward bodies, surrendered
    and buoyant—bodies rising.

AMBISINISTROUS

In what should have been a romantic ruse,
a seductive scheme, the simple shearing
of your harmless hair has us both confused,
your neck nicked and bleeding, me fearing
infection, your wrath, or worse—our passion
sapped by the danger of my clumsy love.
You gasp, then grin, though your face is ashen
as I rush to dab, to press the gauze, to prove
my slip, just that, a slip—not sinister.
If love must leave its mark, then red is fine.
Let it bloom and blaze, let it glow and glister.
My blunder—pure intent—to us a sign
of things to come: at every slip of tongue
or knife, resist the urge to come undone.

RAPTURE

for Devi

The way milkweed pods flurry
on the limbs until rain intervenes.

The way contrails linger like cirrus,
a sigh, a ribbon of breath. The way

a zeppelin floats or a skateboarder
kickflips above the rim. The way ants

crawled out of the banana, still unpeeled,
the *oh* and shine of your gasp, *sweet*

herbaceous miracle, you said, then flung
them over the balcony where they caught

in the current, a momentary failure
of gravity. That summer at the lake, you

stood on the shore puffing your pipe,
not quite oblivious, when your not-yet-three-

year-old girl vanished under the water,
inflatable ring drifting. Glasses affixed,

camera swinging from your neck, you plunged
into the murky silence, water-logged shoes

dragging you down, tobacco flakes rising.
When finally your fingers brushed her belly,

you grabbed her, cradled her to the surface,
hair matted with leaves, fingers clutching

your tie, sweet mouth stealing the air.
The moment relinquished its grief

and glistened, the air a bright cacophony
of wings. The way, even now, as snow

eclipses the trees, you recall it—
and clutch the edge of doom like a wall

that will keep you upright, the *oh* and shine
of your gasp welling up, your lips quivering.

SURPRISED BY JOY

Surprised by chitlins in the salsa,
underwhelmed by evening's empty udder,

residue of spangled breath.
Psst, psst, says the wind in the trees,

rollicking without which nothing is sure.
Intrigued by id's itch, itch, itch and

stunned by unhinged bones.
Exonerated by this tattered hive and that blue splash,

deictic *there-theres*, the last come hither.
Baffled by crows and poplar fluff,

yearnings and oh-so-tiresome epithets.
Jacketed by pinpricks of light. Surprised by

oceanic hum and warble, by grief's clutch and
years sloughing into now. Surprised by joy.

HYSSOP

Purge me with hyssop and I shall be clean.
—Psalm 51:7

Pink delight. Purple haze. Firebird:
spiky flowers tucked in the leaf axils.

Breathe it. Eat it. Steep it for tea.
Expectorant, carminative, antiseptic.

Use it to paint lamb's blood
over your doorpost, cleanse leprous

sores, drip vinegar into the mouth
of the dying savior, cure camphorous

breath, disengage the gossiper.
Sorrows collect in the corners

where the broom doesn't reach.
Mornings falter, unkempt

as the young woman who flags
me down on my country road.

Her name is Freedom, and all she
wants is a shower. I take her home,

cancel my appointment, and let
her bathe and use my brush.

I feed her hot soup and fill a paper
sack with raisins, canned tuna,

a sprig of hyssop, then return her
to the highway where she disappears

in the mist. I drive away, certain
I have entertained an angel.

CHASMOPHILE

I crawled from the wet meat
of the womb to the dark fuzz

of a blanket over my head
to cardboard slitted with holes,

the flashy wheels it contained
lost in tinsel and ripped paper.

An army of coats in the attic
held me captive in musky fur

and naphthalene, a canopy of lilacs
drowsed me, and the high crook

of a mulberry branch muffled
the whirr of my mother's voice.

Family gossip dropped like crumbs
from the table, where underneath

I hunkered amid the stockinged
and lion-pawed legs. In the barn,

I crept through hay tunnels,
seedpods still green and pungent,

the dark so complete I struck
a match, saw no mouse or snake

to filch the air, then sizzled
the flame in spit. How lovely

the absence of light and voice
in a square of space no bigger

than a pout. My breath slowed.
My bones melted as I curled

up—a delinquent smudge—
blind and blissful in not knowing.

IN YOUR OWN IMAGE

for Eavan Boland

You were not yourself.
The fennel feathering in the cup,
the hearts of palm halved
with the blade,
the saucers stacked on the shelf
and your eyes
mirrored gray in the pot's
banged-up belly.
Your knuckles, inflamed from the heat—
they were all you could muster,
the paltry proofs of yourself.
Day after day you quit the self
you were the day before.

And then he came home loose,

piano fingers unclenched
and pocketed for warmth.
He molded your mouth to his,
cosseted your cheek with a sigh.
Such a simple possession!

All you needed
was his abstinent breath
lullabying you to a deep sleep,
a concussion in whose darkness
you felt complete, your *self* at last—
a shape forming in the void
as thin and brittle as a rib.

DO YOU HEAR WHAT I HEAR?

The brain thickens with noise.
A cricket scritches somewhere

in the house, in February, snow
lacing the windows. A dentist's

drill screeches while I shower.
Someone cracks ice from a tray

in the dark kitchen. An endless
sizzle of fish frying. The caterwaul

of rusted brakes on the empty street.
Perhaps the wind of our quarrel,

trapped in my ear, swirls its harsh
accusations. Maybe the neighbor

dreams of sirens or burglars rattle
the latch. Before I drip rose oil

into my ears or stuff them with salve,
earthworms boiled in goose grease,

let me hold fresh loaves, steaming
from the oven, tight against my head.

Let me imagine silence—the violet
unfurling its petals, a pause, stars

pulsing, dew lifting from the grass.
And if this feverish hood fails

to muffle the bones' quiver, then
let me conjure chimes and chants,

cowbells in a distant field, children
singing *a cappella*, the moon ticking

across the sky, a T-shirt fluttering,
a shovel without its burden of dirt.

FENNEL

A fire-flash inflorescence.

Licorice-scent. Feathery leaves.
Fluky seeds, more worm than rice.

Summer sleeps in its pale green bulbs.
        Fleshy globes of gratitude.

No frippery, this one.

Stuff it in sausage, in key-holes
        to repel evil spirits. Rub its creamy
        salve in red-veined eyes.

Swallow it as antidote to death cap
        and rabid dogs. Chew the marathon

seeds in waiting rooms, during dreary lectures,
        at family reunions where your uncle

drones on and on about camshafts and fan belts
        while the roast scorches. Nibble it

to stave off hunger. Get thin with it.

EPISTLE TO THE RATS

If a house is infested with rats, these can be exiled by
the simple process of writing them a letter . . . .
            —William Wells Newell, "Conjuring Rats."
                    Journal of American Folklore, 1892.

I tried to ignore you: the gnawing
inside the wall, the smudged holes,

the chewed shoes and books, ruptured
bags of garbage and rice, the tracks
like curled ash on the snow-drizzled

porch. I christened you: *Rattus rattus*,
Rattus norvegicus, brown rat, black rat,

wharf, sewer, roof rat, zoonotic pest
transporter, tattletale, snitch, lowlife,
rat fink, stoolie, filthy bung, scurvy

companion, lump of foul deformity,
dirtbag, stuffed cloak-bag of guts.

I poisoned you with warfarin to make
you bleed and calciferol to crust
your lungs, but still you clamber up

rusted cans, chew through puttied holes,
take and claw and tear in the darkness,

nest your whiskery nares in our socks.
Now you have scratched into my dreams
bearing a man's face, stubbled and toothy,

and a woman's, your lipsticked pucker
like my grandmother's, and a child's,

fat paws dusted with powdered sugar.
Sleep drags its scaly tail over my chest
and I see a warehouse, no windows,

ghosts inside, pieces of sky floating
to the dead trees, a moth hovering.

And so, Messrs. Rats and Company,
as morning sweeps your skittery snouts
back into your crannies, I lay my stick

down and offer you my lard-infused plea:
You have fed from the scraps of my kitchen

and left your trail of turds across my floors
long enough. I ask you kindly to depart.
Hustle now to my neighbor's barley fields.

Feast on apples dropped from his trees
and snuffle the lilies among his gravestones.

May you find warmth in his cattle's breath,
water from his well, and shelter in the roots
of his tamarack. Hereafter, may you and I

share only seed husks, tufts of fur caught
on the gate, and the hunger that drives us.

SMUG

We roam a roofless city, wander streets
unknown. A vortex of gossip pulses

like a thunderstorm. Death blows in,
wearing his tattered uniform. Spurned

by smoke and acrid boasts, he has yet
to learn the weight of sigh and touch, turn

and counter-turn, the subterfuge of light
at dawn that stills us. We're smug,

too drugged with love to hear the clink
of shovel on stone. Too foolish to flinch,

we refuse to grieve another stillborn tryst.

SHELTER GAMES

A midnight gale blasts shingles
from the roof, slams a yard chair

through the window. You grab a tape
measure, toothpaste, and three tins

of sardines as we head to St. Mary's.
I wake from a nap to find you wrapped

in army blankets with another woman,
her guard dog growling when I speak,

and all you say is *give me a break,*
it's my birthday. I join the old folks

in a bingo game, convincing myself
I don't care, as letters and numbers

plop to the floor. An old woman falls
asleep eating spaghetti; I scrape a noodle

from her face. The wind dwindles
and the fire marshal says we can leave.

I circle the room with my eyes shut
against your birthday glee, groping

the walls for an exit. I crouch in a dark
closet so static and quiet that I begin

to calculate the ratio of systole to exhalation
and classify molecules by color. I decide

that wind is better than stillness, the way
it repositions the familiar—the chair

wedged in the window, me here, you there
with a woman who can't see your face—

the way it tatters what we think is ours.

THE SPACE BETWEEN: 4 A.M.

The angel, the one you knew in fourth grade,
slips in, quiet as the scent of gardenia. She's

the skinny one, her off-key hum soothing
as a purr when she counted the broken bones—

four—in your left hand. Now she has heard
your summons, the chaos of whispering

in the corner. The crumpled note the night
he left. The ground too soggy for burial.

She crosses her legs, taps her ancient fingers
as though she's bored, but you ignore her,

concentrate on the daddy longlegs dangling
in the window, the refuge of cold tea, the smack

of the *Times* against the front door—anything
but her imposing glare. She understands

the weight of night, how it pushes you down
and sits on your chest like the kid who pushed

you off the jungle gym, how it suffocates
you with *what-ifs* and *if-onlys*. Like now—

if only you'd acknowledge her, give her
permission to shush their rants and hustle

their gauzy forms out the door. But hurry.
Soon it will be too late—the light rushing

in, dissolving them in its prism of color,
breathless, if only for a day, until darkness

rouses them again. But you turn her away.
What would you do without their company,

the squabbles that feed you, like gristle
and sour wine, the discordant hum—

if only, if only—that covers you like wet wool?

Breath Sounds

Do not try to be saved, but let Redemption find you, as it certainly will. Love is its own rescue; for we, at our supremest, are but its trembling Emblems.

—Emily Dickinson

BREATH SOUNDS

Babies Hospital, Inc.
Wrightsville Beach, NC

My clunky white shoes squeak
with animal sounds as I wheel

the ultrasonic nebulizer down
to the ward, its walls cheery

with pink rabbits and red ponies.
Here, the poor kids slub blankets

sticky with Jell-O, their parents
forty miles away curing tobacco.

Ivy sleeps through breakfast,
spit bubbles swelling with each

wheezy breath. Rudy, oblivious
to the IV in his scalp, stacks blocks

on his bed. I wipe noses, percuss
chests, adjust oxygen tubes snaking

to green tanks. I pretend to look
for Cora, hiding behind the nurse's

desk or under her bed, then lunging
at me with a squeal and incessant coughing

when my back is turned, her arms
poised for a hug. I hold her for a full

minute, press my lips to her salty
skin, her chest struggling to expand,

her laughter mucked with mucus.
Taped to the wall beside her bed

are crayoned pictures of a scruffy
dog named for her dead brother

and lungs shaped like upside-down
broccoli, alveolar sacs smudged with yellow.

I lead her back to the treatment room,
fit the mask over her mouth and nose.

The machine heaves its foul breath
into her lungs, acetylcysteine's stink

of rotting onions. The sticky aerosol
glints in the fluorescent light. Cora

tickles my wrist between inhalations,
one more game of touch, before ripping

off the mask and tossing it. It tastes
bad—her only complaint after years

of hospital stays, injections, weeks
without seeing her family. I equip

her with pen and paper. She writes:
Dear Mr. Mucomyst Maker: Onion

is not a flavor that will cure my cystic
fibrosis. Cherry would better clear

the mucus from my chest, and please
if you change it, I'll never ever again

tease the nurses or throw up on the floor
or complain about the medicine I know

will save me. But they couldn't, he wrote
back, his letter tucked inside a box

of cherry suckers, arriving three days
after Cora's funeral. I return to the ward

where I listen to every sigh, pant, gasp,
and wheeze, every cough sputtering with life.

FROM *GERARD'S HERBAL*:
OF BORAGE

Bee bread. Bugloss. Starflower.
Italian, *boragine*. Spanish, *boraces*.

Pliny calls it *euphrosinum*, as it makes
a man merry and joyful. Gallant blue

flowers. Use them in salads to exhilarate
and make the mind glad, to drive away all

sadness, dullness, and melancholy. 'Tis good
against swooning, cardiac passion, falling sickness.

Make a syrup, adding thereto powdered bone
of a Stag's heart, to quiet the lunatic person.

Ego borago gaudia semper ago.
I, Borage, bring always courage.

HOUSE OF SCLEROSIS

in memory of David Citino

Gurgling with bourbon, you fall down the stairs
and crack a rib. You laugh yourself to bed.
You nick your chin while shaving and tear
a muscle shooting hoops. When you shred
the cheese and a fingertip, stub your toe,
or scald your tongue, you don't hesitate
to blame the dog, the snow, the squawking crow
or even—clever chef—something you ate.
In time, you shed the scab and pesky limp—
you flee the house of pain. And me? I fall
into atrophied chairs, the light so dim
I can hardly see, the phone dead, the walls
and insulation frayed. I'll take the blame.
I'll stay. The anger here clamors my name.

TISSUE

for my mother

As though to convince us she's still game,
my mother pulls from her coat pocket
a lemon, blue with mold, and tosses it,
a perfect serve, to the ceiling, Her eyes
glimmer, for just a moment, and she's

back on the court, thirty–love, muscles
poised to swing, but the lemon thuds
to the floor, and she falters, then crumples
to her chair, here but not here, the threads
of her brain tangling into hard knots.

She arrives at the table singing *Jesus loves
me* and lavished with every necklace
and bracelet she owns—pearls, garnets,
silver charms twinkling on her chest
and arms—but no skirt over her worn slip.

She shushes us, her conniving daughters,
for whispering secrets behind her door,
then for two hours she stands at the sink
and scolds us, scrubbing the disposable pan
we used and tossed in the trash to save time—

nothing goes unclean in her kitchen.
Now, she occupies herself with toilet paper,
gently tearing off each square, folding it first
in half, then in quarters, and stacking them,
hundreds of pink and green squares, corners

painstakingly aligned in five-inch pillars.
She arranges them in bowls and wicker baskets,
on window sills and under her bed. She assembles
them like sentries next to the china teacups—
for special occasions, she says, never certain

when the king of Nepal may show up for dinner.
We leave the stacks, undisturbed, grateful
for what she hasn't lost: her need for order,
the folding of grace in her lap, the gifts
her hands still know how to make by heart.

MULBERRY

Scrawny legs dangle from a branch
thick with serrated leaves

whimpers muffled by gnats and heat—
the smell of anger and overripe fruit

fermenting—red stains in the dirt
and a paper sack: pink pj's, saltines,

three apples—a bike tossed against
the trunk, snapped chain dangling—

and the squirrels, apathetic as stones,
drunk with heat and rotten fruit.

THE BANKER'S WIFE CROONS FEAR

for Katherine

1. Xanthophobia: Fear of Yellow

It began with the buttercup held
under her chin, yellow glowing
like saffron until the honeybee

lodged its stinger, then buzzed off
to die. Was it ever cheery, this pallid
smear between orange and green—

the six-point star sewn on every
Jewish sleeve, the dog's jaundiced
tooth, the infected haze corrupting

the window, the egg's oozing eye?
Yellow ghosts nudge her awake,
cover her mouth with crime tape.

She finds rest in curtains drawn
against the sun, dark glasses, music
drifting in shades of blue, a black

and white TV. She knows the trade-off:
the sun's sultry breath or pale curls
sliding through her fingers for days

blurring to gray, the smell of damp
papers, her husband's antiseptic voice
slogging the day's deflated numbers.

2. Katsaridaphobia: Fear of Cockroaches

Not the wolf spider on the vine,
not the centipede in the cellar,
not the silverfish on the tub,
not the earwig in the laundry,
not the millipede in the mulch,
not the stinkbug in the fruit bowl,
not the weevil in the pancake mix,
not the beetle in the Persian rug.
But the cockroach, only once,
tangled, hissing, in her hair.
Her husband weighs the cost of systemic
destruction, but only for a moment.

3. Phobophobia: Fear of Fear

What if her neighbor's ball strays
into the ooze dripped from the belly

of the garbage truck? And the invisible
germs—staph, strep, E. coli—swarm

the ball, then his hands, his mouth,
his eyes, his brain? What if the parsley

and potato skins she stuffed in the dark
hole of the sink spawn new growth? What if

she didn't melt teaspoons of sugar to check
for slivers of glass, check and re-check

the dial tone, the oven, the locks? What if
she didn't wear rubber-soled shoes to change

light bulbs or wipe her toilet seat with alcohol?
She pads each step, counts each breath

of noxious air, wills her body sealed,
a perishable locked against contagion.

He brings her plastic flowers, water filters,
air filters, antiseptic, and toothbrushes

by the dozen, buys policies against earthquakes
on odd days (cost effective, he says), installs

railings and motion lights. Still, she finds death
in the currency of smell, asphalt after rain,

and touch, his gentle squeeze, and words,
probability and *perceived risk*. It's the little

things, she says, what you don't expect,
like the microscopic bugs infesting our flesh.

My skin, my skin—how can I ever crawl out?

EPITAPH FOR A HOUSEKEEPER

After W. H. Auden
for Marlene

Cleanliness, of a sort, was what she was after,
And the ditties she composed were tough to understand;
She spotted pretension like dust on a gloved hand,
And was hardly enthralled by Armani or fleets
of Fraser yachts. When she cried, politicians erupted in laughter,
And when she died, schoolboys flicked their butts in the streets.

THE UNDERTAKING

for Beth, Joan, and Robin

The doc called the bright spot
on the scan a tumor, though I

squinted to see it in the lower right
corner of the screen, which was,

he said, the lower, outer edge
of my left breast. The cells,

mutant, out of control, no contact
inhibition. After the surgery—

after you left—I wore a camera.
A Nikon dangled over the left side

of my chest, filling the space
emptied of tissue. My lopsidedness

had purpose, distraction. I snapped
the world in black and white.

The bronze horse in the park.
Ice crusting the bay. Storms

of startled pigeons. I ate alone.
Worked alone. Hiked the labyrinth

of city streets alone—my own
contact inhibition, a healthy state.

I didn't blame you. I missed it,
too, the breast, imperfect though

it was. When you said you could
"handle" it, we laughed. But at

the fourth week, when I carried
laundry down the basement stairs

without your help, you said it
wasn't the breast you missed,

but the symmetry, the evenness.
It was your "aesthetic sensibility"

that failed us, and you left.
Now I'm learning how to conjure

color and beauty, the speckled
petal of an orchid, a splash of peach

and mint, an owl's random hoot.
When I curl up in the darkness,

its amnesiac embrace erases you.

FROM *GERARD'S HERBAL*:
OF ANGELICA

Root of the Holy Ghost, hot and dry
in the third degree. Leaves divided

into other leaves, snipt about. Hollow
stalks, seven foot high, jointed or kneed,

and tufts of whitish flowers. The root,
thick and oilous, out of which issues

an oily liquor, a reasonable savour,
not much unlike *petroleum*. A singular

remedy against poisons, plague, all
infections taken by evil and corrupt air.

If you take but a piece of the root
in your mouth, or chew the same

between your teeth, it drives away
the pestilential air. It is available,

as Fuchs says, against witchcraft
and enchantments. It cures the bitings

of mad dogs and other venomous beasts.

AN ADMONISHMENT OF BOYS

for Miranda

And then the melting,
    the sound of hyacinths

opening, sorrow dripping
    from the eaves, borders

of light expanding. Spring,
    a script you don't want

to read. A pie on the porch
    you won't eat. The boy

returns. He stuffs beer cans
    and butts in your hedge,

as though no one lives there.
    Dark yard, dark house.

He brings a friend, their
    laughter admonishment

you bristle against. You wonder
    if his chin stubbles yet,

if he thanks his mother
    for clean shirts or finds

the dirty magazines his father
    hides in the tool box.

You wonder who will teach
    him to spell and swim

and pray and savor crumbs?
    To release the hair

from his comb to the birds?
    To separate the woolly

milkcap from the morels—
    to know its poison?

How will he learn to keep
    his hands to himself?

You bolt your house against
    the swelling light, against

the pornographic smell
    of pansies and the pie,

persimmon this year, that I
    leave on your doorstep.

THE BLUE CLOAK

1.

I refuse the map. Forgo the sturdy shoes.
I shrug off the ragged water of the past.
My antipodal star riffs like the blues.
I step double-time across the bones and vast
landscapes of asphalt and stubble. He woos
me still, and waits, declares he'll be the last.
His words flutter like ashes in the wind.
For once, I run away, free, undisciplined.

2.

Only the sun holds still, over the bay,
its blue penumbra both morning and night.
The town itself bristles, a busy spray
of flaw and folly. One man, full of spite,
flings feathers to the wind; a woman sways
her friend with gossip. Yet no one incites
the other to anger. There hangs the knife,
and there sighs the man with his cheating wife.

3.

But now I humble back, the music lost
along the bank, the horses chuffing clouds,
caves quiet. My muddied soul sighs *what cost,
what cost*—but we all descend, don't we, cowed
by hunger, thinning hair, and years varicosed
with backfired plans. Let's rest, let's disavow
our pockets of bone, voices from the past.
Let's sink into our own delight at last.

FROM *GERARD'S HERBAL*:
OF THE ARTICHOKE

Cinara, of *cinis*, ashes,
wherewith it loves to be dunged.

With deep gashes in the edges of leaves,
with a gutter along the middle, having no

prickles at all or very few, and a stalk
bringing forth a fruit like a globe, opening

to a flower of all thread, gallant purple.
If you mark the trough in every leaf,

it shall appear that the Creator in His
secret wisdom did ordain these furrows

for no other purpose but to guide the water
which falls off, unto the root. The nails,

that is the white and thick part in the bottom
of the outward scales, and the middle pulp,

whereon the downy seed stands, are a dainty
dish and good to procure bodily lust.

Moreover, the root, if boiled in wine
and drunk, is good against the rank

smell of the arm-holes, for it sends
forth plenty of stinking urine, whereby

the rank and rammish savour of the whole
body is much amended.

SUPPLICATION

Which of you, if your son asks for bread, will give him a stone?
Or if he asks for a fish, will give him a snake?
—Matthew 7:9-10

I asked for an orange, a handful of almonds.
    You fed me cold meat and gristle.

I asked for a cottage facing the morning sun.
    You carried me to a cave in the mountain's
    craggy heart.

I asked for the sky, an open scroll, tatted with lace.
    You plunged me, dreamless,
    into the phosphor.

I roamed the desert looking for bread.
    You led me to a broom bush
    with paltry shade.

I planted asters and forget-me-nots.
    Onion grass and cockleburs overran
    the garden.

I asked for an angel, ecstatic and untethered.
    You sent a heavy-hooved donkey. I nuzzled
    my face in her ears. She called me an outlaw.

I waited for thunder and fire-crack, for sorrow's ashes.
    You awed me with babies. When they cried,
    I cried. When they slept, I heard a still small voice.

I asked for remedy, balm, anodyne.
    You gave me a warm cup, a sturdy table, a room
    chirping with crickets. You fed me poems.

What the Wind Said

Surprised by joy—impatient as the Wind.
—William Wordsworth

WHAT THE WIND SAID

Psithurism: the sound of wind in the trees

We've all heard it, the scorn of rain
on the roof, the fuss of forgotten sheets
on the line, the *psst*, *psst* of pine needles
tapping the pane. But this time, the wind

barges in, burgling the gloom I've nestled
into, scattering the silence and shuffling
the torn-off calendar days pyramided
on the desk. She breathes my shape

into the shirt hanging on the chair,
then drops it on the floor, sets frames
askew, gilds the room in corn dust
and feathers. Her silky skirts swoosh

by my bed, her snickers and *tsk*, *tsk*s
collect in the corners. True to her windy
self, she ruffles and marks everything
as hers, no line taped to the floor

dividing what's mine and what's hers,
all of it sliding beneath a watery blue
wave. My heart thumps *almost*, *almost*.
I grip the sheets and close my eyes,

ambling from this room to the dream's
snare: a baby tumbling through a chute
from sky to earth, and each time I'm almost
there to catch him, bystanders *tsk*, *tsk*ing

their disapproval, the baby whooshing
out to who knows where, and I wake
up to the same old grief hunching over
me, luring me back to limbless sleep.

But now, stirred by the rumple and whirr
of air in motion, the scruffy yowl, the prism
of red and purple quivering on the wall,
I rush to claim him, arms spread wide as wind.

FIRST STAR

A sign. You stagger after it,
   shedding your coat,

then the weight of your boots.
   Someone follows you,

stepping in your frosty prints,
   carrying a shovel. Breathe

the light; your breath shimmers.
   Soon he will fall back.

The star changes neither size
   or position. You pause.

It's not the star you want
   but what its light grazes:

grass flattened by a boar,
   swoop of a screech owl,

rusted-out Chevy bursting
   with sumac and feral cats,

the light scattering its intractable
   logic on every blue leaf

and tuft of fur. You know
   the bear is back, trampling

your tomatoes and squash as you
   now hunger for anything

that gleams, a counterpoint to cold,
   and you don't begrudge him

his fill. You reach the open field,
    where margins bleed to black,

trees shadow-humped, air quivering.
    You lie on the ground to look:

your star's lost in a blazing sky.

LIFE GOALS

Let's begin with twilight tweaker,
forest ranger, big city foot-courier,
ramekin washer, antique duster,
living mannequin (coiffed and windless),
peanut packer, hem presser, skeet shooter,
mattress tester, ash artist (portraits only).
I would have settled for egg flipper,
blue hair shampooer, hay stacker,
collector of pure (so many dogs!),
snake milker, mud lark, barn mucker,
leech collector, sin-eater, tick tweezer—
anything, O beloved, O grandest dame—
anything but this: your thistle, your dread,
your thirst, the creases in your forehead.

INTERFERON

Three hours after the needle
stick in one or the other thigh,

alternating each week
to confound the bruising,

I crumple in a frozen field,
my breath curling in crescents.

A magpie cleaves the darkness,
then pecks the side of my head,

accusing me of sleeping.
My bones shake against my will.

My skin no longer fits, stretching
and stinging as I try to climb out

of it, but I can't lift myself high
enough. Field mice gnaw my toes.

The clouds' heavy rasps muffle
my voice, and snow veils my eyes.

I give myself up. Every eyelash,
muscle, nerve, and cell surrendered.

Only one thing will I claim when it
comes at the nadir of this long night—

the scent of almonds or clover,
sometimes tapioca, sneaking in

with the light, sweet molecules
infusing my lungs, nudging me

toward blue linen and clean socks,
my husband's voice calling me back.

FROM *GERARD'S HERBAL*:
OF THE PLANTAIN

Not serpent's tongue, dog's tongue,
or ox tongue, but lamb's tongue,

this one with greater but shorter spikes,
hoary leaves and likewise hairy stalks.

Plantain, Galen says, has a watery
coldness, with a little harshness, without

benumbing. The decoction drunk stops
the bloody fix and all other belly fluxes

in man or woman. Ancient writers found
many good-morrows: that three roots will cure

one grief, four another disease, six hanged
about the neck are good for another malady:

    all which are but ridiculous toys.

A REPRIMAND OF CROWS

for Wanda

You wake to new snow,
    branches bowing

under the weight, yard
    and cobbled street quiet

under a creamy skin,
    not yet ravaged by track

or tire. Who can blame you
    for staying in, refusing

to mar such innocence
    with boot or shovel?

For years, you have welcomed
    only the knife-edge of light

through shuttered windows,
    the muted hum of talk

radio from the extra room,
    the mostly silent phone.

Tires grind in the snow.
    A tire blares. You falter,

breath held, and peer out.
    A Chevy, gaudy red.

A woman steps out, tapping
    her phone with gloveless

fingers. She looks at the ache
    and grit of your house,

the broken mailbox. Snow
    eddies around her face,

sticks to her hair. Fear holds
    you to the floor like spilled

molasses. You will yourself
    soundless as snow,

still as the cemented hearth.
    You will her to leave,

her car to start. You wonder
    who will drive the children

to school, feed the dog, wake
    the husband from his quiet

death, sweep the frozen flies
    from the sill. A truck

screeches its arrival. The driver
    flings the old tire aside,

wrenches on a new one. Finally
    they leave, the moat of snow

to your door untouched,
    its gift of erasure intact,

until the crows return, filching
    twigs and unpicked beans,

flipping snow and *scolding,*
    scolding, scolding the grief

you never forget to feed.

FROM *GERARD'S HERBAL*:
OF MOTHERWORT

Lion's Tail. Heartwort.
Mother's Herb. Pricking husks,

hairy purple flowers compassed
in whorls and little crownets.

Powder the herb in wine
to provoke the monthly course

and cure cramps. 'Tis also good
for them that are in bad travail

with child or likewise with palsy.
The living plant, being of a rank

smell and a bitter taste, profits well
in stony and other barren places.

Motherwort joys to be among rubbish.

FIG TREE

for Dolores

My friend, the scholar, is tucked
in a tidy room on Apple Wood Lane,

the name of her disinfected hallway.
She asks about the baby in my arms,

though all I hold is a book of poems.
She is courteous in her dementia,

uncomplaining as I wheel her around
the potted plants she greets by name—

Walter, Ed, Mary Lou, her eyes
squinting in the fluorescent light.

But the fig tree she remembers: *ficus*,
the sweet fruit she ate in her father's

garden. Perhaps that's where she
is now as she reaches toward

the tree, the puckered leaves
puddling in her lap, but no fruit.

It's that *old bald cheater, Time*,
she says, lucid, her laughter echoing

with Ben Jonson's wit before she
disappears in a haze. The *ficus*

in my living room has never offered
fruit, only shadows beneath flickering

leaves. Its thinning branches gauge
the changes here: my own survival

from state to state, from hitched
to single, from suburb to cramped flat.

I offer it a sigh, but I won't curse it.
Can it endure where I won't last?

Like my friend, I won't grieve time's
cheating. I will buy a stranger's figs,

perishable and whole. Together,
we'll hold the Adriatic weight

in our palms, bite the taut skin,
and swallow the immortal seeds.

EXALTATION

for my parents
White Stone, Virginia

When the two swans return, male and female,
unfolding and flapping in the cool swale,

four years after our mother's noisy last breath
and two years after our father's quiet death,

we know at last they are together once more.
They glide into beauty and unflinching light before

drifting to marsh grass, unruffled, beak to beak,
dabbling for roots, then stretching their sleek

necks into the Chesapeake breeze. And here,
finally, no striving, no squabbling, no fear

of wild dogs, confinement, or time's rough grip.
The last day to call this house ours, we slip

quietly behind the buttonbush for a closer view
and watch cob and pen, as though on cue,

rise in a flurry, full-winged, a crescendo of white,
running across the water, clattering into flight.

A REDEMPTION OF MUCK

It won't swallow you whole.
—Daniel Bonn, *Nature*

for BJ

Years later, you wander alone, find
yourself in muck up to your waist, the small
variations of stress pulling you in.

                But that's it—as far as you'll go,

your flesh less dense than the cold press
of sand and salty water. Cumulus warps the sky.
Pray it doesn't rain.

Peaks and craggy cliffs hover as though weightless.
Pray they don't shift.

Breathe the lovely stench of peat.
Call it penance.

Yet, how could you have known, a child
yourself then, his smile benign
as he watched us swim day after day,
like someone's dad.

At dusk we all hustled out the gate,
our parents waiting, except you—caught up
in the dare, eager to climb on the back
of his Harley. Just a short ride, he said,
just around the block

and you woke up in a field
wet with morning fog, crows pecking
the buttons on your shirt.

You woke up.

And now you're stuck in memory's bog,
limb and root beyond reach, no ragged edges
to clutch, and for a moment

you don't care about tomorrow. You'd like only
to fold yourself in sleep, but look:

The clouds disperse like years.

The sky articulates its slow apology.

                For once, feed on light,
on wind ruffling your hair.

Look back if you must—
it won't swallow you whole—

then wriggle your toes, your strong calves.

Let truth seep in to break the hold
and sift the layers of bone and grief.

Listen: The mourning dove coos
to her mate, or is it someone in the distance

                calling your name?

DIRTY TALK: A MARRIAGE POEM

for Brooker

Shunne obscene borborology, and filthy speeches.
—J. Trapp, 1649

It's not what I want to hear as we spoon—
this rumbling in your gut, the borborygmic
froth of penne and pesto, the tympanic
swoosh of too much fruity ale. The sigh.
The snore. The cricket in your nose. A fluky
symphony of body talk. Such noisy weather.
But never has thunder harmed anyone.

Today I dug up the dirt with my hands,
sifted the crumbly loam for quivering things—
slugs and root-nesting grubs, bristled worms,
sow bugs coiled into perfect brown pearls,
and spent things—acorn crumbs, feathers,
a comb, a rusty spoon, two plastic champagne
cups—my fingers excavating a rowdy history
of our dirt—its grit and muck wedged in the arc
of my nails, smeared across my chin and cheek,
clumped in my hair.
                         So much for dirty talk.

Wade with me in my puddle, my pond,
my creek, my lake, my ocean of bliss.
Splash me. Dunk me. Dive with me into blue
depths of thirst, weightless, deliquescent.
Sink beneath the click and moan of whale song,
the flutter of luminescent squid, the flash
of a hundred glimmering tails, down
to the bottom, where the spoil of our years

settles in the nooks and crannies of wrecks
turned into reefs, where the rumblings of gall
dissolve in the immense wave of desire.
Then pull us both to the surface, gasping,
to the electrified air, your hot breath,
your thunder and noisy weather. I am
my beloved's and my beloved is mine.

PLANTING IN WINTER

As if the unplotted earth, its glint
    and heave, could refuse

the tiller, the hand that starts and stops
    at will. Inevitable wreckage.

As if, when you dislocated
    your left shoulder birthing

your first born, you could *not push*.
    As if the boy down the street,

mute after the fire, could resist
    the bully's taunt. For two hours,

cheeks puffed, he held the robin's egg,
    filched from the nest, in his mouth,

until the small beak pecked and pecked
    the slimy shell, and when the boy opened

his mouth, a whole bird fluttered out—
    more eloquent than speech or song.

You forget how to sleep. Darkness
    quivers with molecules you try

to count. Both gift and curse.
    Under Orion's watch, you trowel

a patch of dirt, plant carraway, butterbur,
    mugwort. As if you can shuffle

stars, swap seasons, rebuff the owl's
    echoing accusation. Remember

that summer when someone's child
    toddled too close to the water's edge

and disappeared in a galaxy of fear—
    how you pulled him out, silvery

and bubbling. This, then, is your miracle
    of sod and bloom: the sage and coriander

sprouting, the fluted angelica rising
    above your head, its umbels like wings

                awash in wonder.

LET WHAT RISES: A CENTO

What lover, what dreamer, would choose
planting: good Lord, worming tobacco, digging
to metaphysical new-mown hay.
Hell must break before I am lost.

I cannot tell the rate at which I travel backwards,
the experience of repetition as death.
There is a landscape, veined, which only a child can see,
struck by window bargains or is it the gift

of a million myths, choreography of wind, wave,
and plastic fantasies of gesture and extension.
The sod itself, not lonely, and immune to death,
has hardened me and sweetened me.

Not everyone knows what she shall sing at the end.
Let what rises live with what descends.

Notes

"Rapture": The banana is a large herbaceous flowering plant in the genus *Musa*.

"Epistle to the Rats": "Filthy bung" is from in *Henry IV, Part 2*, Act 2, Scene 4. "Lump of foul deformity" is from in *Richard III*, Act 1, Scene 2. "Stuffed cloak-bag of guts" is from in *Henry IV, Part 1*, Act 2, Scene 4.

"From Gerard's Herbal: Of Motherwort," "From Gerard's Herbal: Of Angelica," "From Gerard's Herbal: Of Borage," "From Gerard's Herbal: Of the Artichoke," and "From Gerard's Herbal: Of the Plantain" were assembled from entries in the 1633 edition of John Gerard's *Generall Historie of Plantes*, updated by Holly Ollivander and Huw Thomas, Velluminous Press, 2010.

"The Blue Cloak": Some imagery alludes to Pieter Bruegel's painting, "The Netherlandish Proverbs," also known as "The Blue Cloak." Two stanzas appeared as part of a crowd-sourced canto written for the *American Scholar*'s Next Line, Please weekly forum.

"Life Goals": In the Victorian era, "pure collectors" collected dog feces from the streets to sell to tanners for the leather-making process.

"Fig Tree": In the gospels of Mark and Matthew, Jesus curses a barren fig tree.

"Dirty Talk: A Marriage Poem": The closure refers to Song of Songs 6:3.

"Let What Rises: A Cento"
Sources:
Wallace Stevens, "Hymn from a Watermelon Pavilion"
A. R. Ammons, "Auditions"
Marianne Moore, "Tell Me, Tell Me"
H. D., "Eurydice"
Elizabeth Bishop, "The Man-Moth"
Adrienne Rich, "A Valediction Forbidding Mourning"
Adrienne Rich, "Dreamwood"
Bill Knott, "The Golden Age"
David Citino, "Sister Mary Appassionata to the Human Awareness
          Class: Notes Toward the Perfection of Sex"

Amiri Baraka, "The New World"
Robert Pinsky, "An Explanation of America: A Love of Death"
Denise Levertov, "A Ring of Changes"
Mark Strand, "The End"
Edward Hirsch, "Poor Angels"

Acknowledgments

I wish to thank the editors of the following publications in which these poems first appeared:

Briar Cliff Review:
  "Poem as a Field of Action"
Five Points: A Journal of Literature and Art,
2015 James Dickey Prize for Poetry:
  "Dirty Talk: A Marriage Poem"
  "A Reprimand of Crows"
  "The Space Between: 4 a.m."
Measure: A Review of Formal Poetry:
  "Ambisinistrous"
New Millennium Writings:
  "Chasmophile"
  "Fig Tree"
Next Line, Please. *American Scholar*:
  "Epitaph on a Housekeeper "
  "House of Sclerosis"
  "In Your Own Name"
Nimrod International Journal of Prose and Poetry:
  "Tissue"
  "Interferon"
  "What the Wind Said"
  "Do You Hear What I Hear?" (under the title, "Tinnitus")
Ruminate:
  "Planting"
  "Rapture"
Sow's Ear Poetry Review:
  "First Star"
  "Epistle to the Rats"

Special thanks to: Robert Brooker, Ann Bomberger, Carol Hayes, Shreelina Ghosh, and Emma Brooker, generous and attentive readers; Ben Furnish and Cynthia Beard, exquisite editors at BkMk Press; Enid Shomer, esteemed judge of the John Ciardi Prize for Poetry; and M. Scott Douglass, publisher and managing editor of *Main Street Rag*.

Berwyn Moore is the author of two previous poetry collections, *O Body Swayed* and *Dissolution of Ghosts*. As the inaugural Poet Laureate of Erie County, Pennsylvania, she edited the anthology, *Dwelling in Possibility: Voices of Erie County*.

Her poetry has appeared in such journals as *The Southern Review, Shenandoah, and JAMA,* and she has won awards from *Bellevue Literary Review, The Pinch, Margie, Nimrod, Sow's Ear Poetry Review, New Millennium, Briar Cliff Review, Negative Capability Press,* and *Five Points*.

She has worked as a reporter, a freelance writer, and a respiratory therapist. Currently professor of English at Gannon University, she lives in Erie, Pennsylvania, with her husband Robert.

Winners of the
John Ciardi Prize for Poetry:

The Resurrection Machine by Steve Gehrke,
                selected by Miller Williams

Kentucky Swami by Tim Skeen, selected by Michael Burns

Escape Artist by Terry Blackhawk, selected by Molly Peacock

Fence Line by Curtis Bauer, selected by Christopher Buckley

The Portable Famine by Rane Arroyo, selected by Robin Becker

Wayne's College of Beauty by David Swanger
                selected by Colleen J. McElroy

Airs & Voices by Paula Bonnell, selected by Mark Jarman

Black Tupelo Country by Doug Ramspeck,
                selected by Leslie Adrienne Miller

Tongue of War by Tony Barnstone, selected by B. H. Fairchild

Mapmaking by Megan Harlan, selected by Sidney Wade

Secret Wounds by Richard Berlin, selected by Gary Young

Axis Mundi by Karen Holmberg, selected by Lorna Dee Cervantes

Beauty Mark by Suzanne Cleary, selected by Kevin Prufer

Border States by Jane Hoogestraat, selected by Luis J. Rodríguez

One Blackbird at a Time by Wendy Barker,
                selected by Alice Friman

The Red Hijab by Bonnie Bolling, selected by H. L. Hix

All That Held Us by Henrietta Goodman, selected by Kate Daniels

Sweet Herbaceous Miracle by Berwyn Moore,
                selected by Enid Shomer